I LIVE IN DENVER

I LIVE IN DENVER

A GUIDED TOUR OF DENVER'S PAST AND PRESENT

Written and Illustrated by

ELIZABETH NELSON

GREENWICH PRESS

DENVER

Nelson, Elizabeth, 1938-
   I live in Denver / written and illustrated by
Elizabeth Nelson. – 1st ed.
     p. cm.
     LCCN 2001095132
     ISBN 0-9714078-0-0

     1. Denver (Colo.)–History–Juvenile literature.
2. Historic buildings–Colorado–Denver–Juvenile
literature. 3. Art, American–Colorado–Denver–
Juvenile literature. [1. Denver (Colo.)–History.
2. Historic buildings. 3. Art, American.] I. Title.

F784.D457N45 2002   978.8'83
                     QBI01-701068

Production Management by
Paros Press
1551 Larimer Street, Suite 1301, Denver, CO 80202.
www.parospress.com

BOOK DESIGN BY JENNIFER EITEMILLER
BOOK PRODUCTION BY SPUTNIK DESIGN WORKS, DENVER

Printed in Hong Kong
1   3   5   7   9   10   8   6   4   2

Acknowledgments

I would like to thank my husband, Bob, for all his support and help in making my dream become a reality. To Alfie, all of my love and wishes for a long, happy life. I'd also like to thank Andy Cookston of Digital Impact, who always went the extra mile. My many thanks also go out to Jennifer Eitemiller, whose graphic designs created the first phase of "I Live in Denver" and helped me to visualize it as a book. To the many helpful assistants in the History Department of the Denver Public Library who manage and maintain the records and photographs that made this book possible – I thank you. It's easy to see why the Library was voted number one in the nation! In compiling "I Live in Denver," I came to appreciate the founders and present-day contributors who have worked tirelessly to make Denver the unique, exciting city it is today. For their generous and unselfish efforts I am grateful.

I dedicate this book to my husband, Bob,
to my children Julie, Laura and Martin,
and to my grandchildren Stuart and Emma.
A special thanks goes to my little muse, Alfie.
May we all stay forever young.

TABLE OF CONTENTS

Welcome to Denver as it was long ago.

We have a proud history that we'd like you to know.

When you came to our city you'd arrive at the station,

Where trains would roll in from all over the nation.

There was a fine arch to welcome you here,

So all who would come would be filled with good cheer.

The Welcome Arch at Union Station was dedicated by Denver Mayor Robert Speer on July 4, 1906. It was his intention that the Arch would last for many generations. It had the word "Welcome" written on both sides, but in 1908 one side was changed to read "Mizpah." As visitors approached Union Station getting ready to board the train to leave Denver, they would read the word Mizpah which is from the Bible and is Hebrew for "The Lord watch between me and thee, when we are absent one from another."

The Arch was 65 feet tall and 80 feet wide and was garnished with over 2,000 lights. Imagine what a beautiful sight it must have made for all to see! In the Mayor's dedication speech, he said it was "an expression of the love, good wishes and kind feelings of our citizens to the stranger who enters our gates." I think that Denver has always been the kind of city where we are friendly and do our best to make all visitors feel welcome.

Unfortunately, sometimes progress brings change and this was the case for the Welcome Arch. In 1931 the Arch was removed because people believed it was getting in the way of all the new cars on Wynkoop Street and the cost of the electric bill for the 2,000 lights was more than the city was willing to pay at that time.

There is a movement afoot to return the Arch to Union Station, so perhaps some day when you come to visit Denver it will be there in all its former glory – we can only hope!

This was our Capitol a long time ago,

A year when we had a very big snow.

Horses and carts hauled the snow away,

While children gathered together to play.

Our Capitol looks much the same today,

Though the trees have grown tall and the drugstore moved away.

Have you ever wondered why the Capitol building is located where it is? Well, in 1874 Henry C. Brown, a prominent citizen who also built the Brown Palace Hotel, donated 10 acres of land for this purpose. Before this gift there were two other proposed sites: Golden, just west of Denver, and Colorado City, near Colorado Springs. At this time Colorado (the Spanish term meaning 'red') was still a part of the Kansas Territory. It wasn't until 1876 that Colorado became a state.

The construction of the new Capitol Building did not begin until 10 years later and it took over 22 years to be completed. The original designer of the building was Elijah Myers, but additional contributions were made by Denver architect Frank Edbrooke. Myers predicted that it would be one of the finest buildings in the country. The beautiful dome, which rises to a height of 272 feet, was not always covered with gold as it is now. The citizens of our state objected to the use of copper for the dome because it was not a metal native to Colorado. It was then decided that the Capitol should have a dome of gold. A huge effort was put forth to collect enough gold for the dome, with contributions coming in from all over Colorado. It truly demonstrated the generosity and pride of our early founders. The miners donated over 200 ounces of gold needed to gild the dome, which was completed in 1908. In 1950, the dome was in need of repair. Again, the citizens of Denver came to the rescue and collectively donated over 50 ounces of gold for the repairs.

The House of Representatives and the Senate are located in the State Capitol, and the Governor's office is also here. Only 35% of the building is used for offices; the balance is purely decorative. There is an impressive marble staircase leading to the upper floors and on the first floor there are eight beautiful murals by artist Alan True, accompanied with verse by Thomas Ferril. They effectively tell the evolving story of Colorado and the West.

The illustration is of the State Capitol in the year 1913, when there was a huge snowfall. Flurries began on December 2nd and by the 5th over 45 inches of snow were on the ground. Large horse-drawn carts were used to carry away the snow. It was truly a White Christmas!

One of my favorite times of the year

Is when it gets cold and it snows here.

We have a park where, long ago,

You could put on skates, get on the ice and go.

When you got cold there was a gazebo there,

Where you could keep warm with hot chocolate to share.

Now it is gone but the spirit is kept

Of all the good times that the skaters left.

The Ghosts of Sunken Gardens will always stay,

Because their memories were special and we'll keep it that way.

This scene is titled "The Ghosts of Sunken Gardens" because of all the memories of the good times that must have taken place here. Sunken Gardens was part of an effort around 1910 to make the City of Denver a more beautiful place to live. It is located on the west side of the city at 9th and Elati. Previously, the site had been a garbage dump and was a terrible eyesore. Sunken Gardens was a huge improvement for the community. A lake was built that could be used for swimming in the summer and ice skating in the winter. Hundreds of colorful lights were arranged around the perimeter of the water to enhance the beauty of the park. They would twinkle automatically in alternate colors of red, white and blue. Can you imagine a summer night in Sunken Gardens?

During the winter the lake would be used for ice skating and was illuminated on evenings when the skating conditions were good. The Westinghouse Company presented the City of Denver with a lovely Moorish-style pavilion where people could put on skates and warm themselves in winter and keep cool in the shade in summer.

Later, the park was embellished with an array of flower beds and trees (some of which may still be there!) for all to enjoy. In 1926, West High was built, just west of Sunken Gardens. It is a beautiful backdrop for this lovely park. The east side was bounded by Cherry Creek, and still is.

It is now the turn of another century and, as time will have it, all things change. The lake is gone and the pavilion has long been removed, but Sunken Gardens and West High School are still an important part of our community. This beautiful place is filled with lovely memories from the past. Happily, there is a citizens group which is making a tremendous effort to renovate the park and recapture its past. Sunken Gardens has a reputation as one of Denver's beauty spots.

Have you ever heard of the Unsinkable Molly Brown?

She was a famous lady who lived in our town.

She was strong and courageous, she knew how to survive

And in a shipwreck tragedy she helped many to stay alive.

When she came home to Denver she was welcomed with cheers

And has remained our hero for years and years.

This is the house where she used to live;

She was a special lady who knew how to give.

This beautiful house at 1340 Pennsylvania Street was the home of the famous "Unsinkable Molly Brown." Molly was born Margaret Tobin and her real nickname was Maggie; she received the name of Molly from the movie industry.

Maggie was born in Hannibal, Missouri on July 18, 1867. She spent her childhood with her family in Hannibal, but when she was 18 she heard about men striking it rich in Colorado and dreamed she would be rich enough some day to take care of the people she loved. She hoped that she would marry a rich man and thought that Colorado might be the place to find him, so in 1886 she moved to Leadville, Colorado. It was here that she met J.J. Brown, a miner, and soon thereafter they became husband and wife. Although J.J. was not a rich man at the time, they were happy and both worked very hard. James got his chance when one of his mines struck gold and in a short time Maggie and J.J. were millionaires.

Soon afterwards, they moved with their two children from Leadville to the home at 1340 Pennsylvania in Denver. Maggie was always a lady who cared and was very active in several charities; she was always looking for a good cause where she could lend a hand.

Maggie loved to travel. She was an adventurer and many stories about her were spread around Denver. It did not offend her to be the object of gossip; on the contrary, she loved the attention! After one of her trips to Europe, she decided to return to the States on a new, "unsinkable" ship, the Titanic. It was the ship's maiden voyage and, sadly, disaster struck when the ship hit an iceberg and sank. Many people lost their lives but some, including Maggie, were saved. In her usual spirit, Maggie kept up the morale of the survivors in her lifeboat. She gave some of her clothing to the women and children and encouraged them to keep rowing, because she knew this would help them to stay warm.

She returned to Denver a hero and continued throughout her life to help others. Her memory stays alive in this beautiful house which was lovingly restored and is cared for by Historic Denver. You can visit the Molly Brown House when you are in Denver and experience the elegance of those bygone days.

23

ow we are leaving Old Denver and the things that have passed

Through our beautiful arch, which, sadly, did not last.

It was in front of Union Station for all to see,

And I wonder if you can pick out which one is me.

In 1931 it was removed from our city,

Which most of us think was really a pity.

Engraved on the top of this amazing gate

Was the word 'Mizpah' that in Hebrew will state,

"The Lord watch between me and thee,

When we are absent one from another."

This is the side of the Welcome Arch that you would see as you entered Union Station to board a train leaving Denver. The Arch was built in 1906. When it was first built it said "Welcome" on both sides, but in 1908 the side facing departing travelers was changed to read the word "Mizpah," which is from the Bible and can be found in Genesis 31:49, "The Lord watch between me and thee, when we are absent one from another." When people came to visit Denver they would see this impressive Arch and they would ask what this inscription meant. Some Denverites with a sense of humor would respond that it meant "Howdy" in Indian. I am sure that they were not able to fool very many people!

This beautiful Arch was designed by a female high-school student from East High, who won a contest for her creation. The Arch was a bronze-coated structure weighing about 70 tons; it was built by Denver Iron and Wire Works. The Arch was covered with more than 2,000 lights and at night it brightened the Station as the gateway to the city. There were so many lights around Denver that some citizens thought it was looking a little gaudy. Still, Denver was gaining a reputation as "The City of Lights."

In 1931, the mayor at the time decided to remove the Arch. He reasoned that the cost of the electric lights was too high and it also had become an obstruction to all of the new cars on Wynkoop Street. There has recently been a movement to return the Arch to Union Station. We can wish them well in their efforts; it would be wonderful to see this magnificent structure restored to its previous glory.

When you visit Denver in modern times,
You will fly into DIA,
    where the sun always shines.

It's a beautiful sight
    from your airplane to see,
Like big white tepees
    waiting for you and me.

Imagine the times when Native Americans
    hunted buffalo here;
I often feel that their spirits are near.

When the Denver International Airport was planned, its peaked roof was intended by the designers to create an impression of the nearby Colorado Rocky Mountains, but it has always reminded me of a Native American village filled with beautiful white tepees. What do you think? The airport was built on land that the Indians passed through from time to time as they followed the buffalo herds across the prairie. To honor and show respect for our past cultures, the city officials called upon a Medicine Man to bless the land and clear it for its new use, the new Denver airport. Prehistoric plant and animal fossils and Native American artifacts were found while excavating the site for the foundation of the airport. This tells us a lot about the land and those who lived here long before our time. There has been some talk about returning a buffalo herd to this site, as in the past. How exciting it would be to fly into Denver and see these magnificent animals grazing in the fields surrounding the airport!

Denver International Airport opened in 1995. It covers an area of 53 square miles and is one of the largest airports in the world, with 5 active runways and the tallest control tower, at 327 feet, in North America. There are 23 farms that still work this land, earning as much as $3 million annually to contribute to the support of DIA.

When you ride the shuttle train through the tunnel on your way to board your plane you will see exactly 5,280 propellers that represent the altitude, in feet, of the Mile-High City of Denver. Do you think that you could count all of them? If so, you would have to count very fast! On your ride back to the central terminal you will feel what it must have been like to be in an old gold mine. You will see many mining picks like the ones that were used by the gold miners of Colorado. Did you know that gold was first discovered in 1858 in Cherry Creek where it meets the Platte River? This began the Colorado Gold Rush and the growth of the City of Denver that brought many new people seeking their fortunes. Some people believe that you can still find gold in Cherry Creek if you look closely and are patient.

When you arrive at the main terminal and go to collect your luggage there is a surprise for you. In the Baggage Claim area on the 5th level, snuggled in a suitcase high above the doorway are two fierce-looking gargoyles. One is on the east side and one is on the west side. Perhaps you already know that gargoyles have been placed on buildings for centuries to protect them from harm. I am sure that these creatures will help your baggage to arrive safely - I know that they have watched over mine! Next time you are at the airport it will be fun to look for these little friends.

In the middle of the City there was
a surprise for me –
An Ocean Journey that travels
to the sea.

You'll see sharks and seals
and amazing fish,
And a seastar who may even
grant you a wish!

It's so exciting to spend the day
With underwater creatures in
this remarkable way.

When you come to Denver
you may want to start
At Ocean Journey, it will capture
your heart.

Ocean Journey began as an idea of a husband-and-wife team, Bill and Judy Fleming. They wanted to create a world-class aquarium with a natural environment. They came to Colorado, Judy's home state, to make this dream a reality. After nine years of hard work and overcoming numerous obstacles, Ocean Journey opened its doors on June 21, 1999.

Ocean Journey is located in the middle of the City of Denver on the banks of the Platte River. It is surrounded by Six Flags/Elitch Gardens, The Pepsi Center Arena, Invesco Field at Mile High and The Children's Museum. In the center of fun and activity, it is the only million-gallon, world-class aquarium between the West Coast and Chicago. We are very lucky to have this facility so we can learn the amazing truths about the various life forms that inhabit our earth on both land and sea. In fact, it is the goal of all those who work and volunteer their time at Ocean Journey "to create experiences that inspire our guests to discover, explore, enjoy and protect our aquatic world."

Ocean Journey has over 300 different kinds of fishes, mammals and birds, with a population of over 15,000 living creatures. One-third of the fish are in fresh water and two-thirds live in salt water. They have everything from sharks to tigers spread over five major exhibit themes. You will experience the thrill of standing so close to the aquarium that you will feel as though you can just reach out and touch a shark! You will learn about endangered species and you will see giant pre-historic fossils. You will even feel the excitement of being in a flash flood! As you follow the different exhibits, you will be able to experience the exotic water worlds as if you were there in the water with all the beautiful and unusual life forms.

One of the favorite exhibits is the Sumatran Tigers. It is so interesting to be able to see them in their natural river environment. It looks, feels and smells as it would if you were to visit the tigers in their native country of Indonesia. They live in the hot, humid rain forests and keep themselves cool by swimming and resting in the river near waterfalls.

Ocean Journey is a great attraction in our city; it is truly an adventure you will want to experience whether you live here or are visiting Denver. There is so much to see and learn that you will want to visit Ocean Journey again and again.

I live in Denver and,
perhaps you know,
It's a Mile-High City
where the wind blows and
the snow glows.

We celebrate the Holidays
with visions of light –
To everyone's joy and
perfect delight.

As the magic of the night
slowly appears
We turn on the lights and
everyone cheers!

The City and County Building of Denver is a central part of Civic Center Park. The first structure in the Park was the State Capitol Building. In 1917, as part of a movement to beautify the City of Denver, the Greek Theater was built in Civic Center Park. The many outdoor concerts that were held there attracted large crowds. The Theater was a success and was a beautiful complement to the large gardens that had been built in 1914 as the nucleus of the Civic Center Park.

It wasn't until 1932 that construction of the City and County Building was finished and the Civic Center completed as it is today. It was the work of 39 architects and was designed in the classical style. The bell tower is one of the most outstanding features of the building. It is capped in bronze and has a six-foot, gold-plated eagle standing atop the tower. The building is used as the formal seat of our local government.

Long before the completion of the City and County Building, Denver decorated several of its prominent structures for the winter holidays. As early as 1907, Denver began to line its streets with decorative lights and drape the street lamps with holly wreaths. Large spruce trees were tied with ornate lights on 15th Street. By 1909, the Chamber of Commerce had designated Denver as "The City of Lights."

The tradition of lighting the City and County Building at Christmas began in the 1930s and has continued up to the present day. During the Depression they did manage to economize on the amount of lights used and from 1943 to 1945 there were complete blackouts because of World War II. Thanks to the efforts of our citizens and more recently, the Save The Lights Foundation, the lights have stayed on. In early December, there is a formal lighting ceremony and the lights are then turned on every evening until early January.

Since 1975 a new tradition – The Parade of Lights – has become part of Denver's holiday celebrations. There are brilliant floats covered with thousands of lights, creating a magical winter wonderland. It begins at the City and County Building and winds through the streets of downtown Denver.

The brilliantly-lit City and County Building is an incredible sight to children of all ages and is truly Denver's Magic.

The Denver Zoo is the
place to be;
All your furry friends are
there to see.

There are elephants,
monkeys and zebras who
Would love for you to
visit the Zoo.

Which is your favorite
one to see?

Will you point him out,
will you show him to
me?

40

As the saying goes, "Necessity is the mother of invention," and so began the Denver Zoo. It all started in 1896 when Denver's Republican Mayor Thomas S. McMurray was presented with the gift of a small, orphaned black bear. The bear was named Billy Bryan, after William Jennings Bryan, the unsuccessful Democratic presidential candidate in 1896. After a misadventure in which Billy dined on chickens in the City Park farmyard, there were several attempts to find him a new home. When these failed, he was housed in City Park as the first resident of the new Denver Zoo.

In 1898, the Zoo came to the rescue of another animal, the American Bison. At that time, there were only about 2,000 buffaloes left in the United States. The Zoo used almost half of its yearly budget to purchase six buffaloes for $1,000 and added them to the collection of animals at City Park.

The Zoo was beginning to grow and in 1908 another popular exhibit was added: the monkey cage. People came from far and wide to watch the monkeys play in their new home. In 1918 the Zoo opened Bear Mountain; it was the first home for animals that didn't have bars. How nice for the bears to live in a place that was so close to their natural habitat! One can't help but wonder what mischief that naughty bear Billy might have gotten into at this wonderful place! Bear Mountain is now a historic landmark.

We are very proud of our Zoo and its unique roots. Today, the Denver Zoo provides residents of the City of Denver the opportunity to view and learn about animals from all over our planet. We have a world-class animal hospital that has treated such patients as Klondike and Snow, the two polar bear cubs who were abandoned by their mother and were raised from birth by the doctors at the Zoo. Everyone in Denver adopted these adorable cubs in their hearts and watched them grow into beautiful, healthy, adult polar bears. They are now living together happily at a marine park in Florida.

The Zoo is located on an 80-acre site in City Park just east of downtown. It is the most popular cultural attraction in Colorado and I know that it will be one of your favorites.

The City of Denver is a joyful place –
We like to put on our happy face.

We paint our restaurants the color of the sun
And there are always reasons to have lots of fun!

The Art Museum is a jewel in our crown,
A real treasure in this Queen City town.

We hope that you will help us celebrate
The many reasons that Denver is so great.

44

One sunny day the artist was driving in her neighborhood on 12th Avenue in the Golden Triangle and, to her delight, a local restaurant was being painted a beautiful yellow color. The name of the restaurant is Ilios, which in Greek means "sun." How inspiring to see this colorful building right in the middle of the city like a splash of joy! She knew then that she would have to do a painting. She camped out across the street and began to sketch and take numerous photos. Back in the studio, she transferred her impressions onto a canvas. As the painting evolved, the feeling of a celebration began to develop. In her imagination, she could now see a parade of playful circus animals prancing down Broadway in front of Ilios.

The building on the left is known to Denverites as the Evans School. It was built in 1904 and remained a school for some 70 years. At this time the building is empty, but there are plans to develop the property into a Cultural Center. It is located on Acoma Street, one block west of Broadway, which leads to the Denver Art Museum, creating a pathway referred to as "The Avenue of the Arts."

The unusual structure on the right is the jewel in our crown, the Denver Art Museum. When Colorado was still a young state, art lovers organized The Artists' Club in 1893; in the 1920s the club was reorganized as the Denver Art Museum. Ann Evans was one of the leading benefactors and also an artist. She helped to establish the American Indian exhibit, which is still one of the Museum's strongest collections.

The present home of the Denver Art Museum opened in 1971. The structure created much controversy. There were many interpretations of the unique design by Gio Ponti of Italy and James Sudler of Denver. The Museum is a wonderful contribution to our city. In 2000, the City of Denver voted to expand the Art Museum, making it possible to attract and house larger and more important exhibits for our community. The Denver Art Museum is one of our most valued cultural attractions. Because of the planned expansion of the Art Museum it will, sadly, be necessary to relocate our beloved restaurant, Ilios. No matter where it is, we shall always appreciate its contribution to our city.

Elitch Gardens is a great place to play;
Would you like to go? How about today?

There's so much to do and so much to see –
Lots of fun for you and for me.

The roller coaster ride takes you up and down;
From the top of the hill you can see all over the town!

Six Flags began as Elitch Gardens over a century ago when John and Mary Elitch moved to Denver from San Francisco. They bought some property northwest of Denver where they wanted to create a garden spot similar to the one John had worked at in San Francisco.

One of John's friends, P.T. Barnum, owned the famous Barnum & Bailey circus. In the winter he would bring some of his animals to Sloan Lake and when there were extra babies born he would give them to his friend John Elitch. In the spring of 1890, John and Mary opened Elitch's Zoological Gardens. You could enjoy some ice cream from the soda fountain while you listened to the music from the band that played. Soon after the park opened, Mr. Elitch died and Mary carried on with their dream. She loved the animals and had fun teaching them tricks.

Later, she added a theater where many famous actors would perform on stage. New amusement rides became popular attractions - what a wonderful place for the whole family to have fun and enjoy the summer weather! In 1928, they bought a beautiful new carousel. In the following years, Elitch Gardens expanded with more rides and more fun. It has always been on everyone's list of things to do in the summer.

100 years after they first opened, Elitch's moved to the Platte River Valley, where it frames the skyline of Denver from roller coasters, ferris wheels and a multitude of other rides. If you listen closely you can hear the screams and shouts of joy from all of those who, over the years, have spent countless fun-filled days at Elitch's. Elitch Gardens is now owned by Six Flags, but as the famous sign from long ago still reads, "Not to see Elitch's is not to see Denver!"

They say that money makes the world

go 'round –

Did you know there's a U.S. Mint

in our town?

We make the coins and send them to banks,

Who use them for business and send

back many thanks.

The next time you spend your nickels,

quarters, pennies and dimes,

You can thank the Mint workers in Denver

for your good times.

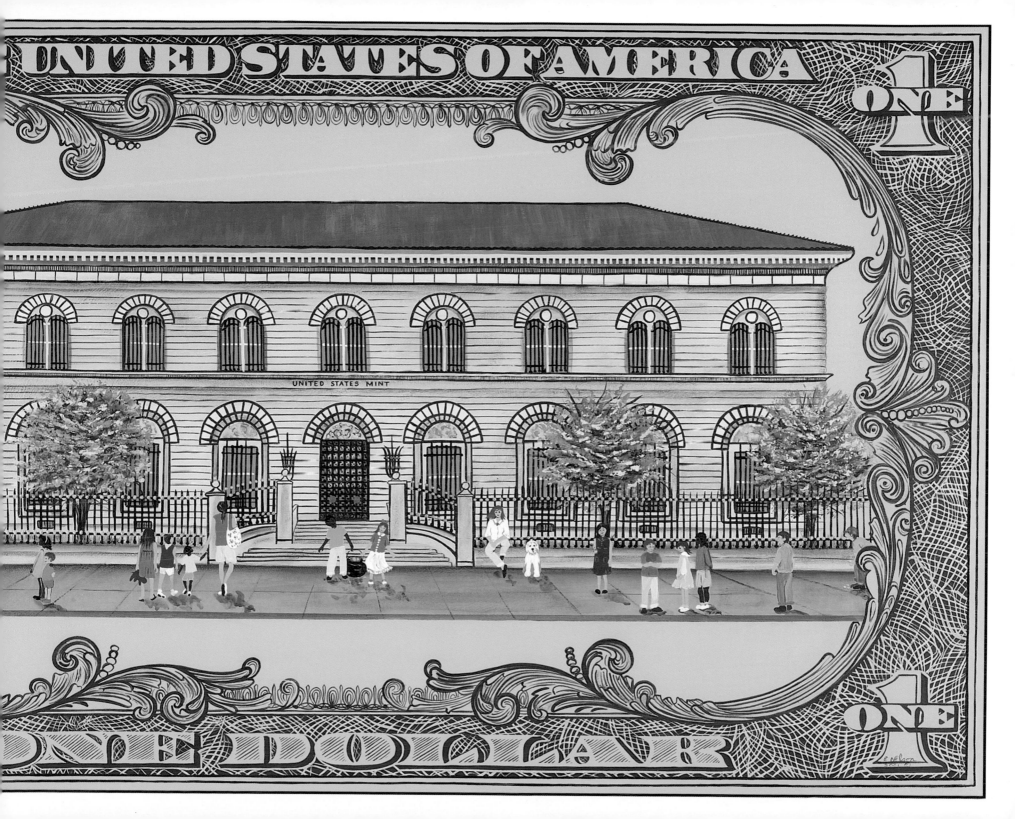

I guess you could say that the need for a U.S. Mint in Denver began with the Colorado Gold Rush in 1858. The dream of finding gold and becoming rich brought thousands of prospectors to Colorado, then a part of the Kansas Territory. In order to purchase supplies, the miners would carry bags of gold that they would use to barter. Some would add fine brass shavings to their gold to make it weigh more, so it became difficult to establish a fair method of exchange.

A Kansas company opened a mint and bank on the corner of 16th and Market Street to mint gold and silver into coins. At this time in our nation's history, it was not illegal for private companies to make coins, as their value was determined by their weight and content of either silver or gold. The Clark & Gruber Bank and Mint opened for business in July of 1860, two years after gold was found on the banks of Cherry Creek. In the beginning, the new mint produced about $18,000 in coins each week.

In 1862 the Federal Government purchased the Clark & Gruber Mint for $25,000 and re-opened it in 1863 as an assay office, where they would test the gold and silver to determine its purity. In the late 1800s, land was purchased on West Colfax for a new mint and the building was completed in 1904. Much attention was given to decorative items in the new mint and many of these features still remain today.

Some of the hallways have the original hand-stenciled and hand-painted borders. The Grand Hall is lined with beautifully-colored marble and original mounted brass wall sconces. The arched ceiling is lit with elegant Tiffany-style chandeliers.

Four U.S. Mints are currently producing coins - in Denver, San Francisco, West Point, NY and Philadelphia, PA. The Denver Mint produces pennies, nickels, dimes, quarters and a new Sacagawea dollar, totaling about 50 million coins in the amount of $6 million per day. In addition to minting coins, the Denver Mint houses one-quarter of the nation's gold reserves, with the rest being kept in Fort Knox, KY and West Point. In 1934, $2.5 billion in gold reserves that had been kept in the San Francisco Mint was moved to Denver; at a later date another $1 billion was transferred. It was felt that Denver would be a more secure site because of the frequency of earthquakes on the West Coast. At today's value, this amounts to about $100 billion worth of gold. The gold was shipped in 75 railroad cars on 25 different trains. When it arrived in Denver at Union Station the gold bricks were loaded onto mail trucks, which were then accompanied to the Mint by police cars with their sirens blaring! What an exciting event that must have been!

A great, glorious American Pie –

What could be better on the Fourth of July?

The weather is hot and it's time to play ball –

Coors Field is the place, near the 16th Street Mall.

Hot dogs and peanuts, goodies galore;

Great fun with the family –

who could ask for more?

Baseball has been a part of our city's history since the late 1800s, but it wasn't until 1993 that Denver's dream of being home to a major-league baseball team was realized. We are the loyal fans of the Colorado Rockies, a member of the Western Division of the National Baseball League. The people of Denver rightly have a reputation for being some of the most enthusiastic sports fans in the world.

From the beginning, it was intended that Coors Field be a community effort. Everyday citizens were invited to be on the Advisory Board and to attend public meetings so that their input could be used in the successful building of the stadium. It was also the desire of its creators that this new ball park reflect the character of the neighborhood. Many of the features of the surrounding historic buildings were incorporated into the design of the new stadium. Even though the structure is new, it has a wonderful, nostalgic appearance. It is truly a beautiful addition to our city.

When you attend a game at Coors Field, you can take in some of the other attractions in the neighborhood. The home of the Colorado Rockies is located in lower downtown, commonly referred to as LoDo. Besides enjoying a meal at one of the many wonderful restaurants in LoDo, you can browse the famous Tattered Cover Book Store, which is located just across the street from historic Union Station. The depot has been a part of Denver's history since the late 1800s. In the early days, many people would come and go through its gates, as it was a center of activity. You may then want to stroll down the 16th Street Mall, a pedestrian walkway that goes from one end of downtown to the other. A short way up the Mall is Larimer Square, where you can relax at an outdoor café and shop in many unique stores and boutiques. Further down the Mall are shops, movie houses and many other interesting sites for you to enjoy.

Coors Field is a beautiful architectural addition to our city and is a popular visitor attraction. The stadium is named for the Coors Brewing Company, which is located in nearby Golden, Colorado.

I guess you're wondering who's been your guide;
For this trip around Denver I've been by your side.

I live in the City; it's a fun place to be –
So much to do and such great things to see.

My name is Alfie; I'm a puppy with flair.
I'm in every picture – can you find me in there?

This is my City and it's a wonderful site,
With a past full of history and a future that's bright.

Denver's a city of fun and good cheer;
Perhaps some day you'll come visit me here.

The Golden Triangle is where Alfie lives. It is a section of downtown Denver that is bordered by Broadway, Speer Boulevard and Colfax Avenue, not far from where gold was first discovered in Cherry Creek. It was gold fever that first brought thousands of fortune hunters to the Mile-High City. Times were hard and the dream of striking it rich was a powerful driving force. Many came, but few were lucky enough to find their pot of gold. Some returned to their previous locations but many decided to stay and make this beautiful area their permanent home. One of the first was William Larimer, who staked off some of the first land of the Colorado Territory and called it Denver, after J.W. Denver, Governor of the Kansas Territory. In the beginning, there were only a few makeshift houses, tents and miner's shacks. As the area grew, Denver and the neighboring area of Auraria became the center of the gold activities.

In 1876, Colorado became a state and the search began for a state capital. The founders decided on Denver. As with most large cities that grow rapidly, there have been many stages and phases right up to today. In the last 50 years, the downtown area has seen major development activities that include the Golden Triangle. Unfortunately, many of the wonderful old commercial buildings and homes were destroyed for parking lots. Thanks to an organization called Historic Denver a great many old buildings have been preserved for present-day Denver. The Molly Brown House is a prime example.

You can't talk about Denver without mentioning the Denver Public Library. The new central library, designed by the famous architect Michael Graves, opened in 1995. Just recently, it was voted the number one library in the nation. Much of the research for this book was done with the help of the librarians of the amazing History Department, on the 5th floor of the Library. These dedicated people have truly kept our history alive by maintaining many old records and making them available to all Denverites.

We hope you've had fun on our guided tour of Denver – past and present. Enjoy our city!

Welcome to the world of artist

ELIZABETH NELSON

Elizabeth with her sheepdog, Alfie,
who can be found in all of her paintings

Elizabeth Nelson paints a fresh, often whimsical view of Denver's most cherished cultural landmarks. Drawing on her extensive knowledge of history and legend, Elizabeth takes a "now and then" look at Denver, enlivening such popular attractions as the Denver Zoo, the U.S. Mint and Ocean Journey, and rejuvenating others — such as Sunken Gardens and the Welcome Arch — that are vivid only in longtimers' memories.

Available framed and unframed, and in a variety of sizes, these beautifully detailed prints offer collectors a terrific way to capture the unique charm and history of Denver. Whether you're a newcomer fascinated by all this city has to offer, or a visitor who wants to remember all the wonderful sights you've seen, this series presents a new look at Denver – both the Denver that existed at the turn of the previous century, and the Denver that thrives today.

Additional copies of this book are available by writing Greenwich Press, 1100 Cherokee St., Suite 303, Denver, CO 80204, by calling 303-573-7399, or by visiting on-line at www.greenwichpress.com.